The Story of the Piñata

Michele Jeanmarie
Illustrated by Mary Sepúlveda

This book is a work of non-fiction. Unless otherwise noted, the author and the publisher make no explicit guarantees as to the accuracy of the information contained in this book and in some cases, names of people and places have been altered to protect their privacy.

Archway Publishing books may be ordered through booksellers or by contacting:

Archway Publishing
1663 Liberty Drive
Bloomington, IN 47403
www.archwaypublishing.com
844-669-3957

Interior Image Credit: Mary Sepúlveda

ISBN: 978-1-6657-6207-6 (sc)
978-1-6657-6824-5 (hc)
978-1-6657-6208-3 (e)

Library of Congress Control Number: 2024912531

Print information available on the last page.

Archway Publishing rev. date: 10/30/2024

The Story of the Piñata

Hanging from a tree is a **piñata**.

Swing to the left.

Swing to the right.

Strike upward.

Strike downward.

Twirl to the left.

Twirl to the right.

Circle all around.

Swing. Swing. Swing.

Across the great seas, journey Marco Polo. He and his crew meet gale force winds that rock the boat.

Back and forth.

Back and forth.

Back to the stern.

Front to the bow.

Right to the starboard.

Left to the port.

As wonky waves toss them aboard, the sailors make it to China.

On arrival, they are more than eager to disembark. Strolling down the narrow passageways, they fill their eyes with many treasures. Farm animals hang from awnings along the marketplace. Marco Polo gazes on. As he peers much closer, he smiles. He realizes they are animals fashioned as clay pots. He enquires about them and learns that farmers hang them in hopes for a prosperous and bountiful harvest. Marco Polo decides to take a few back to his queen, Queen Isabella.

Queen Isabella and King Ferdinand are much appreciative of his gifts. Quite tickled, they encourage him to make more voyages. If clay pots they bring back, imagine what more they can find to fill the coffers. They finance and send him on many more trips across the great seas. Priests are sent with them. They are called missionaries. So called because their mission is to spread the Word of God to others.

Marco Polo and his sailors decide to go another way, this time to India. Sail they sailed, but they did not arrive to India. They arrive in Latin America. They call the inhabitants Indians.

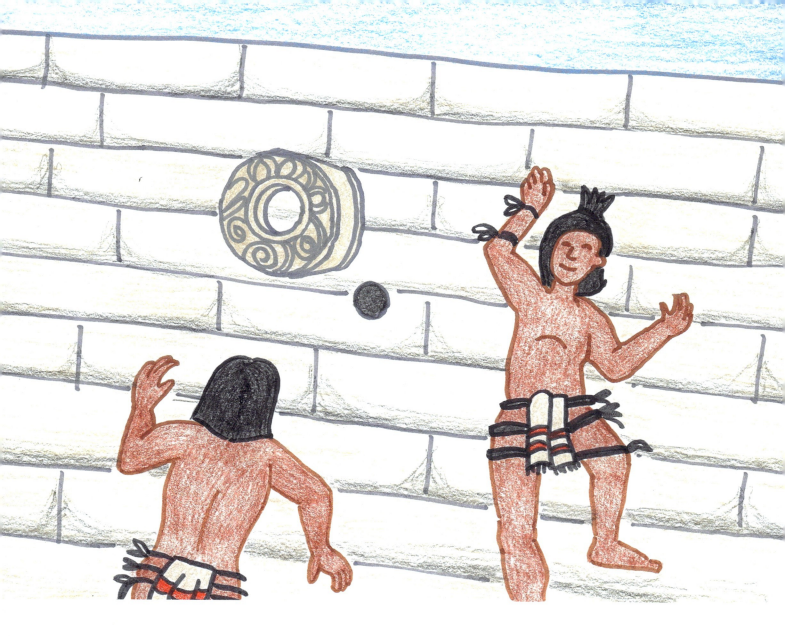

The Indians are very creative. They are vast in numbers. They are very industrious. They are very smart. They are playing a match, on a field very much the length of a soccer field. Hung about midway, up in the air, are two hoops, one on each side, one belonging to each team. The players are using their heads and legs. It is a fast-moving game. To score, they have to get the ball up high, through the opponent's hoop. Not quite basketball, not quite soccer, but an amalgamation of both.

As days march on, the missionaries grow very disturbed. The Indians are dying. The Indians are being maltreated. The missionaries intercede as much as they can. They decide to win over their hearts. They glimpse along the many huts and see clay pots.

Clay pots? They wonder.

They recollect the clay pots they had seen in the palace. With the Indians, they sculpt more of their own. They take some mud and dirt and water and shape them into circles. The circles are named **piñata.** But they are heavy. They carve out some of the mud from the interior.

As they are re-shaping the **piñatas**, they think of the various doctrines they can use to win over hearts.

The sacraments. Of which there are seven.

The deadly sin. Of which there are seven.

The virtues. Of which there are... seven!

They think of adding seven cones to the **piñatas** to represent the seven sacraments:

1. Baptism
2. Reconciliation
3. Penance
4. Confirmation
5. Marriage, **or** Holy Orders
6. Anointing of the sick
7. Last rite

They think of adding seven cones to the **piñata** to represent the seven deadly sins:

1. Greed
2. Gluttony
3. Pride
4. Envy
5. Wrath
6. Sloth
7. Lust

They think of adding seven cones to the piñata to represent the seven virtues.

1. Chastity
2. Temperance
3. Charity
4. Diligence
5. Patience
6. Kindness
7. Humility

To combat **greed**, one is to practice the virtue of **charity**.

To combat **gluttony**, one is to practice the virtue of **temperance**.

To combat **pride**, one is to practice the virtue of **humility**.

To combat **envy**, one is to practice the virtue of **kindness**.

To combat **wrath**, one is to practice the virtue of **patience**.

To combat **sloth**, one is to practice the virtue of **diligence**.

And to combat **lust**, one is to practice the virtue of **chastity**.

The missionaries are covering ground.

A game ensue. To rid the soul of these ailments, the missionaries blindfold the Indians. They hang the 7- cone **piñata**. One at a time, the Indian is spun around thirty-three times, one for each year Jesus lived on Earth. The missionary hands each one a stick.

Blindfold.

Stick quickly is placed in hand.

Spin.

Thirty-three times.

Swing, swing, and swing.

This goes on until the very strong breaks the **piñata** into smithereens.

The Aztecs love the idea and adopt it as their own. In secret, however, they place the **piñatas** on top of a pole of their temple to show gratitude to their own god.

With time, their descendants feature them at Christmas time.

Chela determines that the seven conical **piñata** represents the Star of Bethlehem. Nine days before December 24th, that is, Christmas Eve, the **piñata** rises to stardom. This event is called "Las Posadas," the journey that Mary and Joseph took to deliver Baby Jesus.

Today, the **_piñata_** is made of cardboard, and it is filled with sweets and treats. The **_piñata_** can be found in many shapes, styles, and forms. When the **_piñata_** is busted, everyone scurries to the floor fetching as many treats as possible.

So, have a jolly old time and hit the **piñata**.

Chela watches on, "Let's see, …"

Blindfold, "yep!"

Stick placed in hand, "yep!"

Spin, "yep!"

Thirty-three times…, "n-no. That's too long,

but it was their way to educate them."

Swing, swing, and swing, "yep!"

A song is added.

Everyone sings, as the child swings!

"Dale. Dale. Dale.

No pierdas el tino,

Mide la distancia

Que-hay en el camino.

Que si no le das,

De-un palotazo,

Porque tienes cara

De puro zorillo."

"Go! Go! Go!

Do not lose your balance

turn and turn and turn and

you will find your target

For if you should miss

with a crazy wild swing

You will feel so foolish

that you will run and hide."

A. Guided Reading/ Discussion:

1. We learned there are (7) seven deadly sins: greed, gluttony, pride, envy, sloth, wrath and lust. Why did the missionaries make the Aztecs strike at the 7-conical clay pots?

2. Do you think the missionaries' lessons of striking the (7) seven deadly sins should have been intended for the Aztecs?

   Why or why not?

3. Do you think the missionaries were dutiful in applying this lesson to the Aztecs?

   Why or why not?

4. Do you think the missionaries, in their duty, should have taught the conquistadores the lesson of the (7) seven deadly sins?

   Why or why not?

B. Following are the (7) seven deadly sins:

Lust

Greed

Pride

Gluttony

Envy

Wrath

Sloth

On a separate piece of paper, draw a picture to represent each one, as it pertains to something you may have done. Next to it, draw the diametrical opposite. These are:

Chastity - It overcomes the sin of Lust.

Charity - It overcomes the sin of Greed.

Temperance - It overcomes the sin of Gluttony.

Kindness - It overcomes the sin of Envy.

Patience (meekness) - It overcomes the sin of Wrath

Humility - It overcomes the sin of Pride.

Diligence - It overcomes the sin of Sloth.

Add a caption!

Write your name.

Post.

5. Today, traditions hold that the seven cones, rather than representing the seven deadly sins, now represent the seven sacraments. List.

YouTube, "The **piñata** song," or
"Dale, dale, dale" for music, song, or lyrics.

Design and draw your own **piñata** below.